ANXIOUS

Helping Children Cope With Anxiety

Written by Esther Adler
with Rona Miles

Illustrated by Shrutkirti Kaushal

bright awareness publications ™

www.brightawareness.com

WESTLAKE GAVIN

www.westlakegavin.com

Westlake Gavin Publishers LLC
New York   Toronto   London

For Ben,

Your curiosity, enthusiasm, and determination are an inspiration to everyone.

E. A.

Publisher's Cataloging-in-Publication data

Adler, Esther.
    Anxious: Helping children cope with anxiety / by Esther Adler with Rona Miles; illustrated by Shrutkirti Kaushal.
    p. cm.
    ISBN 978-1632310132
    Series: ColorFeeling
    Summary: Addresses the physical sensations when children feel anxious. Explores typical situations where children might feel anxious. Provides practical approaches to help children cope with anxiety.

[1. Anxious. 2. Emotions.] I. Adler, Esther. II. Miles, Rona. III. Kaushal, Shrutikirti. IV. Title.

First Edition

10 9 8 7 6 5 4 3 2 1

This book belongs to:

_____

Foreword

Anxiety is a complicated and uncomfortable emotion. It has three prongs - emotional, cognitive and physical, which make this emotion multi-layered and difficult for children to navigate. Each of these components encompasses different aspects of anxiety including feelings of discomfort (emotional), thoughts of doom or failure (cognitive), and bodily symptoms such as stomachaches or a pounding heart (physical). These components all combine in a child's heart, mind, and body and make it difficult for them to understand and navigate situations where they experience anxiety.

Oftentimes children are confused when they experience this feeling. They are unsure why they have knots in their stomach, why they sometimes have a hard time sleeping, or why they might be feeling nauseous or dizzy. Teaching children how to recognize this feeling, without even verbalizing it, is important to help children cope with anxiety. In much the same way that we teach a child to recognize the color blue or the letter A, we need to teach children how to recognize the feeling and label it. Doing so is the first step needed in order to help children navigate this challenging emotion. **Goal #1: How can we help children identify the feeling of anxiety?**

Even as adults, we often have a hard time putting into words what we are feeling when we are anxious. We say things like, "I feel nervous", "I have a knot in my chest", "My stomach is churning", "These thoughts are buzzing in my head", "I just don't know what to do with myself". Many times, we get the feeling, but have a hard time accurately putting the feeling into words. If this is the case for many of us, then it is surely the case for little children who don't necessarily have mastery over language or access to certain vocabulary words in order to express their emotions in a nuanced manner. **Goal #2: How can we help children put their feelings of anxiety into words?**

In addition to the uncomfortable feelings that come with anxiety and the difficulty children have choosing words to accurately reflect their feelings, children have an added component: They often have physical pains that accompany feelings of nervousness. I often hear from kids who are anxious that they don't feel well, and many of them describe physical symptoms such as stomachaches, headaches and pain in their legs, when it is apparent that they are dealing with a worrisome situation. These pains often frighten them and take the focus away from the real underlying issue. **Goal #3: How can we help children understand the physical symptoms that often accompany anxiety?**

Finally, once we've helped children identify the feeling of anxiety, put their feelings into words, and also assist them in understanding the physical symptoms that often accompany anxiety, we need to develop ways to help them cope with these uncomfortable feelings. I have always felt that the black and white method of needing to get rid of anxiety never works. We do best when it is approached from a position of reducing anxiety as opposed to eliminating it. **Goal #4: How can we help children problem solve so they can reduce the uncomfortable emotional, cognitive, and physical symptoms that accompany anxiety?**

In the many years that I have spent counseling children with anxiety, I have found that children who are able to recognize and express this feeling have a much easier time regulating their emotions. But not all children can do this easily. For children who experience challenges with recognizing, understanding, and expressing their feelings, it becomes difficult for them to navigate their social-emotional environments. Forming friendships becomes more difficult, school becomes more stressful, and feeling better after a negative interaction takes longer. It is for these children that we need compassionate and patient educators who can use their knowledge and talent to scaffold and help children understand their emotional worlds.

With this in mind, I have always searched for resources to help educators as they help children. And in this quest, I found Esther Adler's ColorFeeling™ series to be an excellent resource. From the inception of her first book *Angry,* through her seventh book, *Motivated,* I have been along for the journey. But her eighth book, *Anxious,* was the one that I had been waiting for because Esther invited me to join her in writing it.

In working with Esther on *Anxious,* it is evident that she has many years of experience working with children as a licensed Mental Health Counselor. She addresses challenges that occur for children in an insightful and creative manner, and I surely learned from her in our collaboration. *Anxious* continues to incorporate all of the qualities that have made the ColorFeeling™ series a success and I encourage you to utilize this resource and to explore the other wonderful books in the ColorFeeling™ series.

Dr. Rona Miles, PsyD, CSP

NYS Licensed Psychologist
NYS Certified School Psychologist

When I feel anxious, my stomach becomes knotted like a gray ball of yarn.

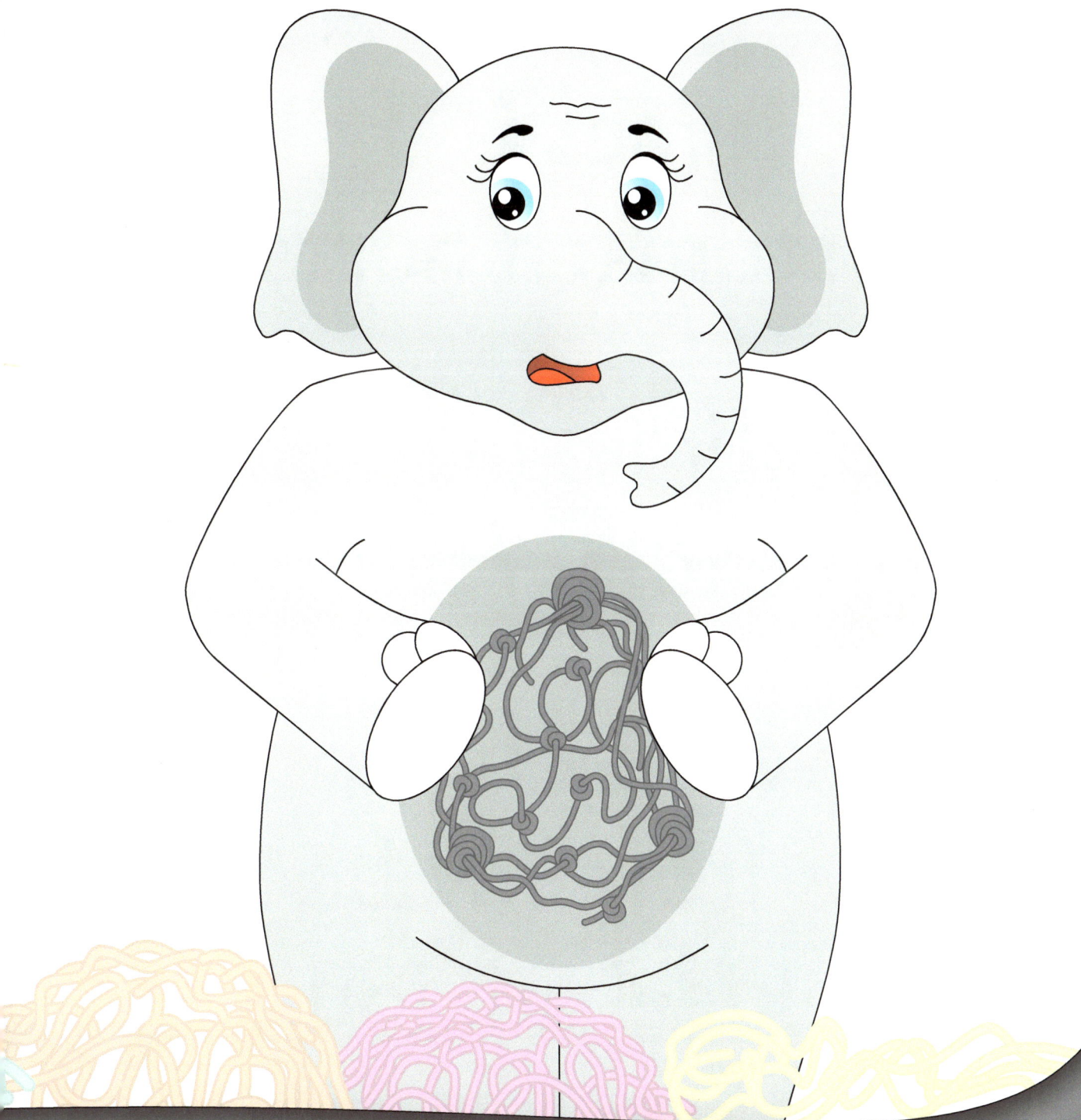

Sometimes
my stomach hurts.

Sometimes
my head hurts.

These may be
signs from my body
that I feel anxious.

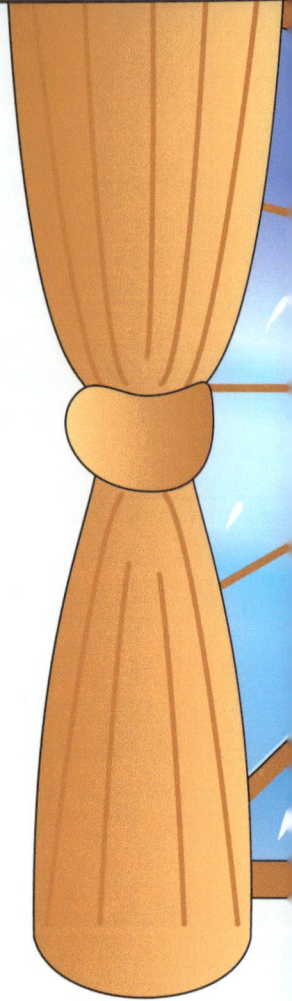

When I feel anxious,
it is the only thing
I can think about.

Anxious, worried, and nervous have similar meanings.

Word of the day:

Anxious = Nervous = Worried

I feel anxious
when people
around me
are anxious.

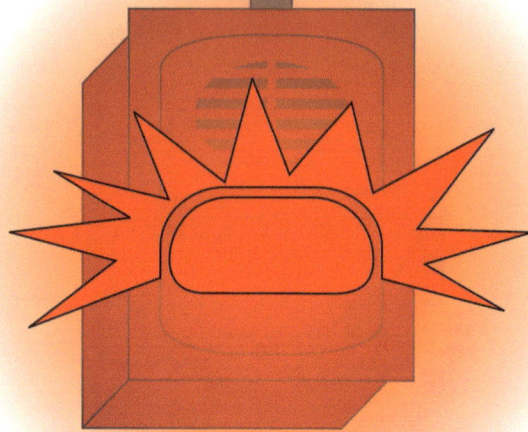

I feel anxious when
I don't know
what will happen.

FIRST GRADE

I feel anxious
when I make
a mistake.

I feel anxious when I have so much to do.

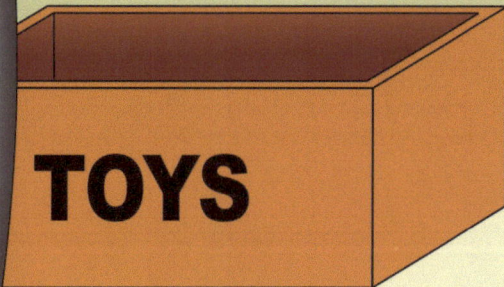

TOYS

Home Work

CRAYONS

List of chores

Do homework

Clean-up toys

Brush teeth

Take bath

Go to bed

Sometimes
I feel anxious and
I don't know why.

Everyone feels anxious at different times. And that's okay.

What makes
you feel anxious?

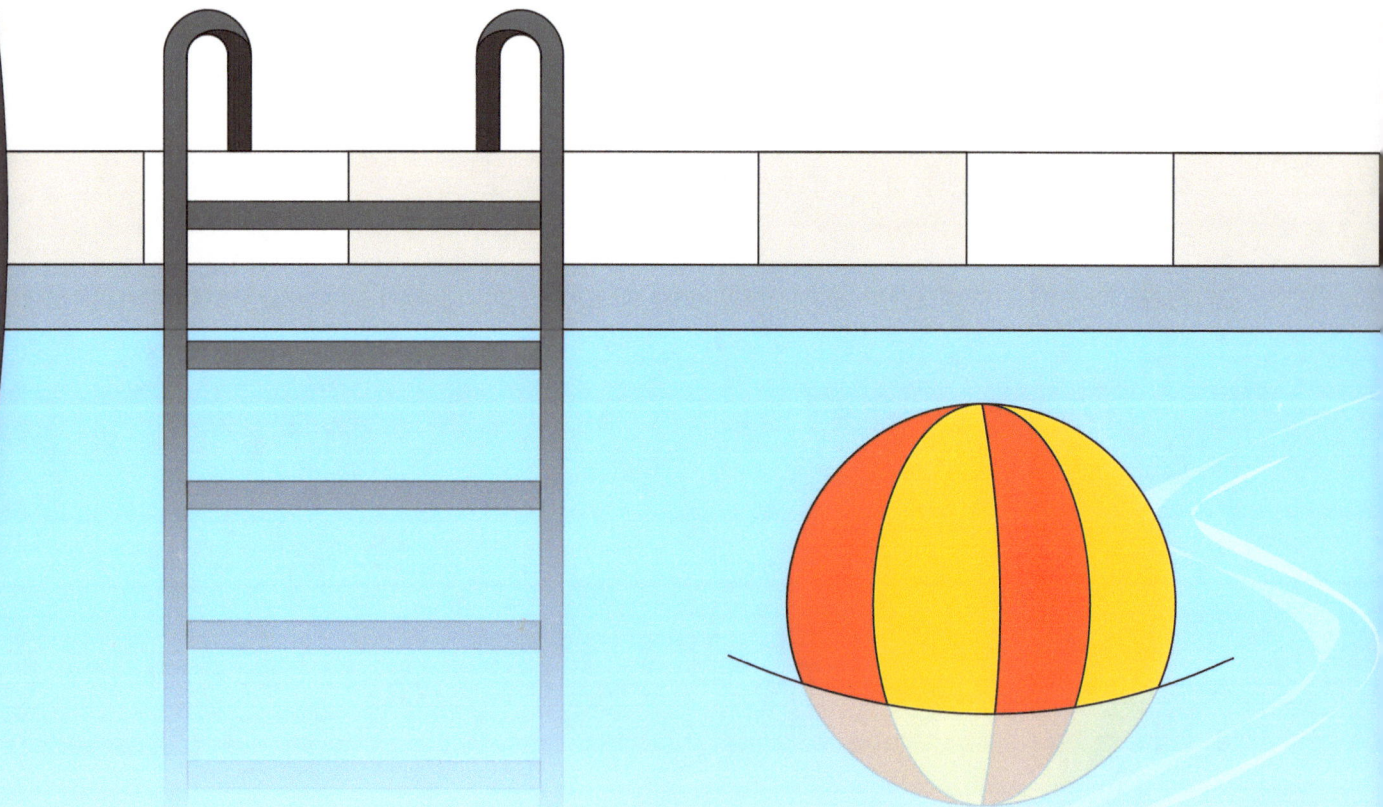

When you feel anxious, what do you want to do?

When I feel
anxious,
I can express
my feelings.

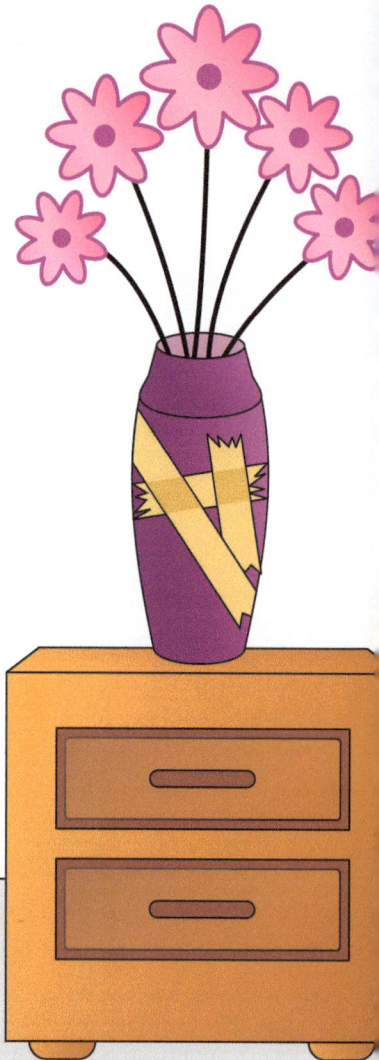

When I feel anxious,
I can take deep breaths
and tell myself
everything will be okay.

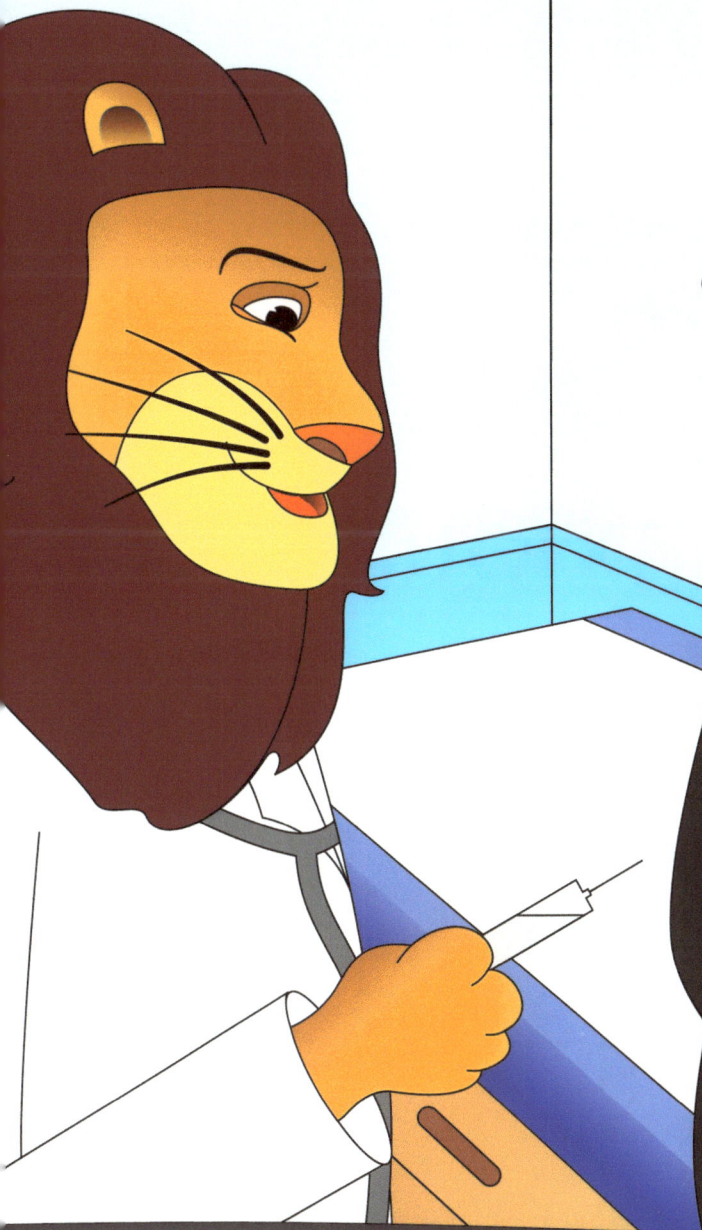

I feel less anxious when I know what might happen and I can be prepared.

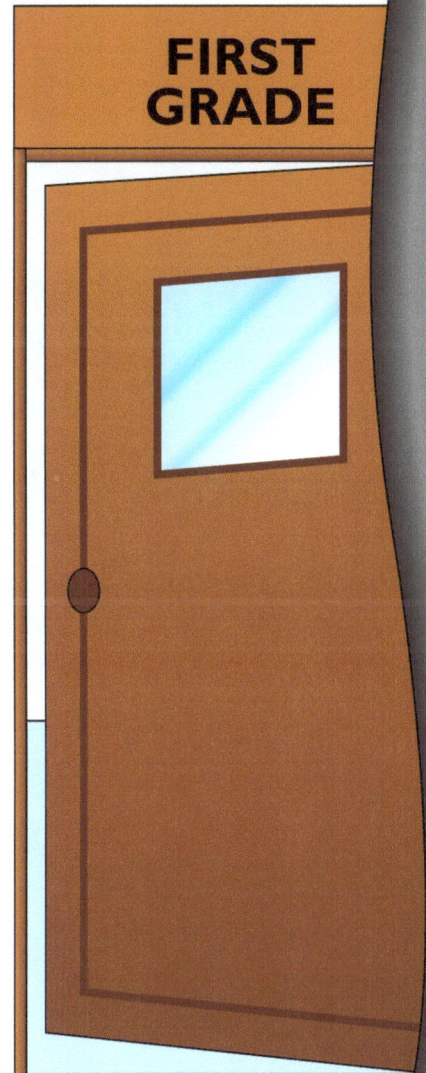

I can draw a picture of a time when I felt anxious.

When you feel anxious, what could you do to feel better?

What makes you feel anxious?
What number would you rate it on the Anxiety Scale?

I feel very anxious when: Anxiety Scale:

1. _____   _____

2. _____   _____

I feel a little anxious when: Anxiety Scale:

1. _____   _____

2. _____   _____

Anxiety Scale

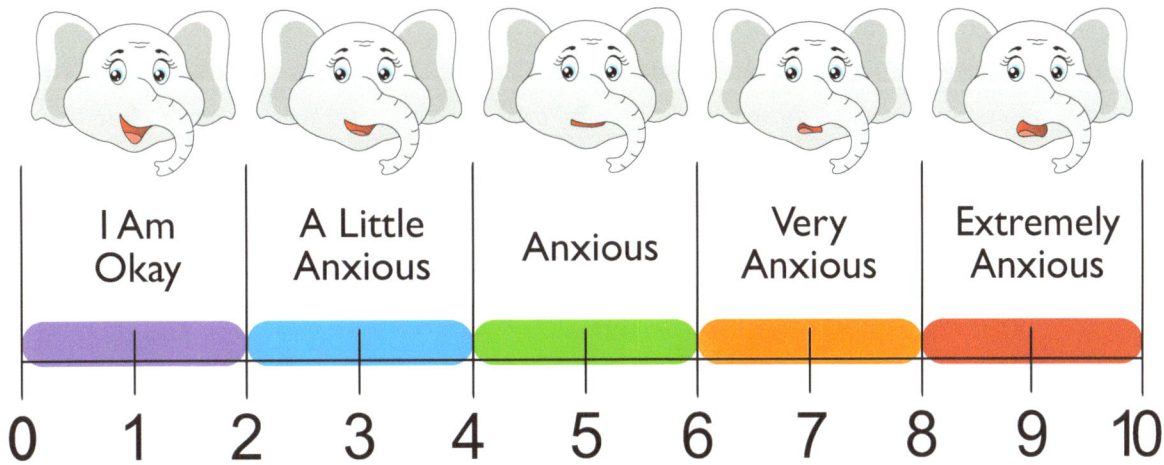

| I Am Okay | A Little Anxious | Anxious | Very Anxious | Extremely Anxious |

0 1 2 3 4 5 6 7 8 9 10

Circle the things that make you feel anxious.

Cross out the things that don't make you feel anxious.

Meeting a new friend	Touching a bug	Sleeping by Grandma's house
Hearing the news	Going to the doctor	Getting a new toy
Playing by a friend's house	Hearing yelling in my house	Making a mistake
Petting a dog	Losing a game	Eating lunch

Tell or write a story about a time when you felt anxious.

_____

_____

_____

_____

_____

_____

Circle what you <u>can do</u> when you feel anxious.

Cross out what you <u>should not do</u> when you feel anxious.

Tell an adult how you feel	Blame another person	Slam a door
Think about times when you felt calm and happy	Listen to music	Take deep breaths
Scream	Hide in a corner	Blow bubbles
Think: "I can get through this."	Ask a teacher for help	Color a picture

What can you do to help a friend feel less anxious?

1. _____

2. _____

3. _____

4. _____

Dos and Don'ts for parents
talking to kids who are anxious:

Don'ts

✘ Don't dismiss your child's feeling.
Example: "There's nothing to be anxious about."

✘ Don't embarrass your child for being anxious.
Example: "Big boys don't get anxious about that."

✘ Don't give a consequence for the anxiety your child is feeling.
Example: "If you don't stop worrying, then you can't come."

✘ Don't get frustrated in response to your child's anxiety.
Example: "I'm getting so upset that you keep talking about…."

Dos and Don'ts for parents
talking to kids who are anxious:

Dos

✔ Validate your child's feeling.
Example: "I see that you're worried about the sleepover."

✔ Empower your child with coping skills.
Example: "Let's practice slow breathing."

✔ Ask your child how you can help them.
Example: "Would it help you if I held your hand?"

✔ Challenge your child's thoughts.
Example: "Remember when you were worried
and it turned out well?"

Asking Open-Ended Questions

One of the best things you can do for your child when they are anxious or worried is to get them to express themselves. A simple way to do this is to avoid asking a closed-ended question and ask them an open-ended question instead. A closed-ended question is one that can be answered with just a single word. An open-ended question or statement is one that calls for a response that includes multiple words and thoughts.

Examples of closed-ended questions:

❌ Were you anxious?

❌ How was school today?

❌ What did you play at recess?

❌ How was the game?

❌ How was your play date?

Examples of open-ended statements/questions:

✔ Can you tell me what happened that made you anxious?

✔ Can you tell me something that happened at school today?

✔ If I would have been at recess today, what would I have seen?

✔ Tell me something that happened during the game that you didn't expect.

✔ What were some of the games you played at the play date?

Parting Thoughts

Anxiety can be a difficult emotion to deal with, but with the proper understanding, tools, and support, your child can be empowered to manage anxiety effectively.

Thank You!

Thank you for using this book as an educational resource. We hope that the book and accompanying worksheets are helpful in supporting children through their worries and anxious feelings.

About the Author

Esther Adler, LMHC, received her undergraduate degree in Psychology and graduate degree in Mental Health Counseling from Brooklyn College of the City University of New York. Esther is a New York State licensed Mental Health Counselor who provides counseling for children of all ages in schools and privately. Additionally, she has training in evidenced-based therapies such as CBT, DBT, and trauma-focused therapy. In her work within the field, Esther saw the need for the ColorFeeling™ series to help children develop a healthy awareness of their feelings. Esther is a mother and grandmother to six children and one grandchild. She resides in New York.

About the Co-Author

Rona Miles, PsyD, received her undergraduate degree in Psychology and graduate degrees in Education and School Psychology from Brooklyn College of the City University of New York. She subsequently received her doctoral degree in School/Child Clinical Psychology from Ferkauf/Yeshiva University. Currently, Rona is an Assistant Professor of Psychology at Brooklyn College, as well as a New York State licensed Psychologist in private practice providing counseling services across all ages. Rona is a mother and grandmother to four children and two grandchildren. She resides in New York.

About the Illustrator

Shrutkirti Kaushal was born and raised in Jodhpur, India. From a young age, she was inspired to draw. She received a diploma in Commercial Art from the Board of Technical Education, Rajasthan and a diploma in Television graphics and Animation from the Asian Academy of Film and Television, Noida. Presently, Shrutkirti is a freelance artist who specializes in illustrating children's books for authors worldwide. Shrutkirti resides in Indore, India with her husband and young son who love to watch her create art.

bright awareness publications™

www.brightawareness.com

- Subscribe to our email newsletter for updates and special discounts.
- Friend us on Facebook for fun contests, coupons, and lots of surprises.
- Download free printables.
- Give us feedback. We love to hear from our readers.
  - ✓ What did you like most about the book?
  - ✓ What can be improved?
  - ✓ Which title would you like to see next in this series?
- Spread the word. Post your review on Amazon.com and other sites.

Visit **www.brightawareness.com** for all the above and more

www.ingramcontent.com/pod-product-compliance
Lightning Source LLC
LaVergne TN
LVHW072124070426
835511LV00003B/85

9781632310132